A PARRAGON BOOK

Published by Parragon,
13 Whiteladies Road, Clifton,
Bristol BS8 1PB

Produced by The Templar Company plc,
Pippbrook Mill, London Road, Dorking,
Surrey RH4 1JE

Copyright © Parragon 1996

Written by Dugald Steer
Series Editor Robert Snedden
Designed by Mark Summersby
Black-&-white illustrations by Richard Hawke

All tartan samples supplied by Lochcarron of Scotland,
Waverley Mill, Galashiels, Scotland, TD1 3BA

Printed and bound in China

ISBN 0-75252-944-7

FACTFINDERS

CLANS & TARTANS

P

∥ • PARRAGON • ∥

CONTENTS

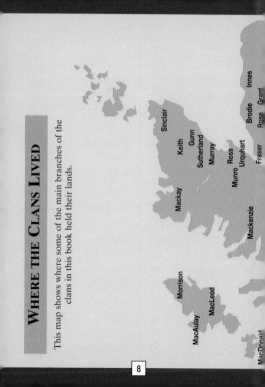

Where the Clans Lived

This map shows where some of the main branches of the clans in this book held their lands.

Morrison

MacAulay

MacLeod

MacDonald

Mackay

Sinclair

Keith

Gunn

Sutherland

Murray

Ross

Munro Urquhart

Mackenzie

Fraser

Brodie Innes

Rose Grant

MacKinnon

Macrae

Macpherson

Farquharson
Anderson Lindsay

Duncan

Ogilvie

MacDonald

Cumming

Robertson

MacDuff

Cameron

Menzies

Macintyre

Macgregor
MacNab
MacLaren

Drummond

Macquarrie MacDougall
Maclean MacCallum
Campbell
MacLachlan
MacNaughton

MacFarlane Graham
Colquhoun Stewart
Buchanan

Ramsay

Livingston

Scott

Elliot

MacEwen
Macfie Scrymgeour
Macmillan
MacNeil
MacDonald

Lamont
Stewart
MacAulay
Stewart

Wallace
Douglas
Hamilton
Kennedy
MacAlister

Bruce

Maxwell

Fergusson

INTRODUCTION

The clan system developed in the Highlands of Scotland during the Middle Ages. It was a tribal system, unlike the feudal system, which flourished in the Lowlands. Whether or not a family owed allegiance to a chief often depended more on where they lived than on ties of blood or marriage.

The clans were made up of a number of different races – Picts from the north, Scots, who had travelled over from Ireland around AD500, Britons from Wales, many of whom had settled in Galloway, Norsemen who settled the islands and the extreme north, and Normans, many of whom came north in search of land at the time of David II, and found it.

This system extended beyond local needs of self defence to embrace the wider politics of the realm of Scotland. Some clans banded together to form federations such as Clan Chattan, others rose to power at certain times, only to have their lands forfeited or taken in battle at others. For a long time the chiefs of the more northerly clans ignored the Crown almost completely. Instead they often gave their allegiance to some powerful local laird. As time went by, power became centralised in the Crown. This process was finally completed after the Battle of Culloden, which marked the real end of the clan system in Scotland. Not all of the clans fought for Prince Charles Edward, the 'Young Pretender' as he was known, yet many did and after the battle a military rule was imposed on the Highlands that was designed to crush the clan system completely. Roads were improved, so that armies could get about the country quicker, and many lairds and landlords, anxious to become rich enough to ape the lifestyles they had seen at the courts of other, wealthier countries, employed English managers, or 'factors', to run their estates entirely for profit. Their actions, and the effects of famines, resulted in the Highland Clearances during which many clansmen were cleared out of their homes and farms to make way for sheep and deer grazing.

Another thing that happened after Culloden was that the wearing of highland dress – kilts and tartan in particular – became outlawed. The tartan patterns that decorated clothing were ancient, but were originally more likely to be associated with a particular area than with a clan, although this often meant much the same thing. During the time when tartan was outlawed many of the old patterns, or 'setts', were forgotten and had to be re-invented during the Scottish Revival of the 19th century. Many clans again took a pride in their names and histories, and chiefs gave their names to tartans – many of which appear in this book.

Note: The tartans in this book are described in various ways – 'ancient' and 'modern' refer to the colours which old and new dyeing processes create, modern dyes being brighter. A 'weathered' tartan looks faded, a 'dress' tartan is used for formal occasions and a 'hunting' tartan is one woven in greens and browns for camouflage.

ANDERSON

Gaelic : Mac Ghille Aindrais
Motto : Stand sure

A branch of Clan Chattan, the Andersons are also known
as the MacAndrews as their name relates them to St.
Andrew, and they have been connected with the Ross
clan, whose Gaelic name is *Clann Andrias*, or Andrew's
clan. Many of the Andersons lived in the region of
Aberdeenshire. A famous Anderson was 'Little' John
MacAndrew, an expert bowman. In 1670 he followed and
killed all but one of a group of cattle raiders from
Lochaber. That man returned home and the Lochaber
men swore to kill him, although they never managed it.

ANCIENT　　　　　　　　**MODERN**

BRODIE

Gaelic : Brothaigh
Motto : Unite

The Brodies are an ancient Pictish family from Moray and they are connected with Scotland's earliest kings. Robert the Bruce gave lands to Michael, Thane of Brodie, in 1311, just before the Battle of Bannockburn. In 1640, the fanatically Presbyterian Alexander Brodie of Brodie led an attack on Elgin Cathedral, destroying many fine paintings and carvings. In revenge, Lord Lewis Gordon burned down Brodie Castle, in Forres, and so the clan records were lost. The rebuilt castle is now owned by the National Trust for Scotland.

ANCIENT HUNTING

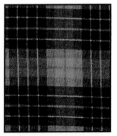

MODERN RED

BRUCE

Gaelic : Brus
Motto : Fuimus *(We have been)*

Robert de Bruce was a Norman knight from Brix in France who came to England in 1066. His son became Lord of Annandale when David I became king, but gave up his lands when David declared war on England. At the Battle of the Standard in 1138, Robert's son took his own son prisoner. The Bruces gained their claim to the kingship of Scotland when the 5th Lord married David's great-granddaughter. The famous Robert the Bruce became king in 1306 and defeated the English at the Battle of Bannockburn in 1314.

ANCIENT

MODERN

BUCHANAN

Gaelic : Canonach
Motto : Clarior hinc honos
(Brighter hence the honour)

The Buchanans are a Pictish family from Strathclyde and the name Buchanan comes from the Gaelic *both-chanain*, which means 'canon's house'. Their lands lay around Loch Lomond, opposite the island of Clairinch, which was used as a gathering place for the clan during wartime. The island was first given to Absalon of Buchanan by the Earl of Lennox in 1225. It is now a nature reserve. James Buchanan (1791-1868) was the fifteenth President of the United States.

ANCIENT

WEATHERED OLD

CAMERON

Gaelic : Camshron
Motto : Aonaibh ri cheile *(Unite)*

The name Cameron probably comes from the Gaelic *cam shrun*, a crooked nose. At one time the Camerons were subjects of the Lord of the Isles, and they fought for him under their chief, Donald Dubh, at the Battle of Harlaw in 1411. At Harlaw they fought alongside the Mackintosh clan, but an argument over land led to a feud with them that lasted for more than two centuries. Sir Ewen Cameron (1629-1719) killed the last wolf in Scotland. His grandson, Donald Cameron, the 'Gentle Lochiel', was wounded at Culloden in 1746, but escaped to France.

MODERN

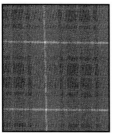

HUNTING

CAMPBELL

Gaelic : Caimbeul
Motto : Ne obliviscaris *(Forget not)*

The Campbells, known as the 'race of Diarmid' from a legendary Scottish hero, have always been a powerful clan. Their name comes from the Gaelic *cam beul* which means 'crooked mouth'. They held lands near Loch Awe from the 13th century and the Argyll Campbells descend from Sir Colin of Lochow, who was knighted in 1280 and was known as Great Colin or *Cailean Mór*. Ever since the chief has always been called *Mac Cailean Mór*. A later Colin Campbell was made Earl of Argyll by James II in 1457 and the 10th Earl was made a duke in 1701.

ANCIENT

CAMPBELL OF ARGYLL

CHISHOLM

Gaelic : Siosal
Motto : Feros ferio
    (I am fierce with the fierce)

In the 14th century Robert de Chisholme inherited a title
and lands as the Constable of Castle Urquhart on Loch
Ness. On becoming Sheriff of Inverness, Sir Robert also
inherited lands in Moray. By the 17th century the clan
chief had come to be known as *An Siosalach*, or the
Chisholm. The clan fought for Prince Charles at
Culloden, where the chief's son was killed by cannon fire.
After the battle, three of the 'men of Glenmoriston', who
helped the Prince to escape, were Chisholms.

MODERN

WEATHERED HUNTING

CLAN CHATTAN

Gaelic : Clan Gillacatan
Motto : Touch not the cat but a glove
(Touch not the cat without a glove)

Clan Chattan, the 'clan of the cat', is really a federation of some 17 clans, all descended from the clan founder, Gillechattan Mor. The chiefship has often been disputed. In 1291, Angus Mackintosh, the head of the Mackintosh clan, became Clan Chattan chief when he married Eva, the daughter of the previous chief who had no sons to follow him. The Macpherson clan believed that their head should have been made chief, and a feud began that lasted for more than two centuries.

CLAN CHATTAN

COLQUHOUN

Gaelic : Mac a' Chombaich
Motto : Si je puis *(If I can)*

In the time of Alexander II, Humphrey of Kilpatrick was given the barony of Colquhoun in Dunbartonshire, from which the family takes its name, by Malcolm, Earl of Lennox. In the 14th century the clan acquired the lands of Luss through the marriage of Sir Robert Kilpatrick to the 'Fair Maid of Luss'. The Macgregors attacked the Colquhouns at Luss in 1603, and were outlawed as a clan by James VI after massacring the Colquhouns and their chief at the Battle of Glenfruin. The Macgregor chief and 11 of his principal clansmen were hanged.

ANCIENT

CUMMING

Gaelic : Cuimean
Motto : Courage

Robert de Comyn came to England in 1066, becoming
Earl of Northumberland in 1069. His grandson married
the granddaughter of King Donald Bane and their son
became Earl of Buchan. By 1286 the Comyns, or
Cummings, were a very powerful family and, in 1306,
Robert the Bruce met the Comyn chief, John, 'the Red
Comyn', in a Dumfries church to talk about their rival
claims to the throne. Robert stabbed John Comyn and
his followers finished him off. As king, Robert tried to
destroy the Comyns, taking away most of their lands.

MODERN

MODERN HUNTING

DOUGLAS

Gaelic : Dubhghlas
Motto : Jamais arrière *(Never behind)*

William de Duglas, lived at the end of the 12th century. His grandson, who was known as 'the Black Douglas', was Robert the Bruce's right-hand man at the Battle of Bannockburn. Later, he died in Spain fighting the Moors while taking Robert's heart to the Holy Land. The family split into two branches when the title Earl of Douglas was taken by the Black Douglas's illegitimate son, Archibald the Grim, and that of Earl of Angus was taken by the illegitimate son of the previous earl, the Black Douglas's nephew, William.

ANCIENT

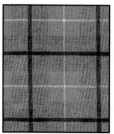

MODERN

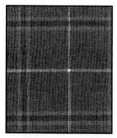

DRUMMOND

Gaelic : Drummann
Motto : Gang warily *(Go carefully)*

A man called Maelcolum Beg, or Little Malcolm, is the first recorded Drummond. Robert the Bruce gave his grandson lands in Perthshire as a reward for spreading caltrops – spikes for crippling horses – at the Battle of Bannockburn. Margaret Drummond married David II in 1369, while Annabella Drummond married Robert III. Another Margaret Drummond was to have become the wife of James IV but was poisoned, with her sisters, in 1501. The Drummonds lost their estates after the Battle of Culloden, but regained them in 1785.

MODERN	DRUMMOND OF PERTH

DUNCAN

Gaelic : Clann Dhonnachaidh
Motto : Disce pati *(Learn to suffer)*

The Duncans are descended from the ancient Earls of
Atholl. Their name comes from Donnachadh Reamhar,
Duncan the Fat, who led the clan at Bannockburn in
1314. Adam Duncan of Lundie was the son of a Royalist
during the Jacobite rebellion of 1745 and joined the navy
in 1746. He became commander of the North Sea Fleet in
1795 and managed to blockade the Dutch coast for two
years. He won a brilliant victory in 1797 at the Battle of
Camperdown and was created Viscount Duncan of
Camperdown by George IV in 1800.

ANCIENT

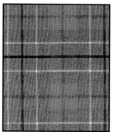

MODERN

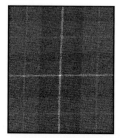

ELLIOT

Motto : Fortiter et recte
(With strength and right)

The Elliots were originally a Borders family. The chief
branch were the Redheugh Elliots but eventually the
Stobs branch inherited the Redheugh lands. One of them,
Gilbert Elliot of Stobs, known as 'Gibbie wi' the gowden
garters' was convicted of high treason in 1645 for plotting
against the Catholic Duke of York. However, the
Protestant King William of Orange later made him Lord
Minto. General George Augustus Elliot defended
Gibraltar against the Spanish and French between 1779
and 1783 and was made Baron Gibraltar.

ELLIOT

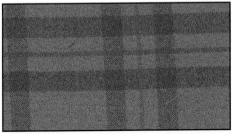

FARQUHARSON

Gaelic : MacFhearchair
Motto : Fide et fortitudine
    (By fidelity and fortitude)

The Farquharsons are Celts and their founder was
Farquhar, son of Alexander Shaw of Rothiermurchus.
They are important members of Clan Chattan. One
Farquharson, Finlay Mor, carried the royal standard at
the Battle of Pinkie, where he was killed in 1547. Anne
Farquharson, wife of the Mackintosh chief, was known as
Colonel Anne or 'La Belle Rebelle' after raising her clan
while her husband was fighting for the Government and
later ambushing men sent to capture Prince Charles.

FARQUHARSON

FERGUSSON

Gaelic : MacFhearghuis
Motto : Dulcius ex asperis
(Sweeter after difficulties)

The various branches of the Fergusson clan are probably descended from different ancestors who were all called Fergus. The Fergussons of Craigdarroch are descended from a 12th-century Fergus who founded the Abbey of Dundrennan. The Fergussons of Kilkerran trace their ancestry to John, Son of Fergus, who lived at the time of Bannockburn. Other Fergussons claim that they are descended from Fergus Mor MacErc, a king of Argyll. The Perth Fergussons are the principal Highland branch.

ANCIENT

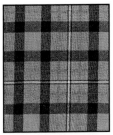

MODERN

FORBES

Gaelic : Foirbeis
Motto : Grace me guide

The story goes that the first Forbes was a man called
Oconochar, who made his home in the 'Braes o' Forbes'
after killing the fierce bear that lived there. In any case
we know of a John of Forbes who had lands in Forbes in
the 13th century. The Forbes clan became Protestants,
supporting the Government during the Jacobean risings.
Duncan Forbes, Laird of Culloden, convinced many clans
not to join Prince Charles. His family still aided their
Catholic relatives, hiding Alexander Forbes, 4th Lord of
Pitsligo, after the Battle of Culloden.

MODERN

MODERN DRESS

FRASER

Gaelic : Friseal
Motto : Je suis prest *(I am ready)*

The Frasers were a Norman family from La Fraselière in
France and a Simon Fraser had lands at Keith in 1160.
Another Simon Fraser beat the English three times in
one day in 1302 at Rosslyn. Captured, he was executed in
London. Alexander Fraser married Robert the Bruce's
sister after Bannockburn and the Frasers of Lovat are
descended from his brother Simon. Their chiefs are
always known as *Macshimi*, the son of Simon. Simon
Fraser, 11th Lord Lovat was executed in 1747 after
Culloden, the last peer to be beheaded.

ANCIENT HUNTING

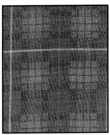

MODERN RED

GORDON

Gaelic : Gôrdon
Motto : Bydand *(Remaining)*

The Gordons were an Anglo-Norman family and had lands in Berwickshire by the 12th century. Adam of Gordon was a follower of John, the Red Comyn, but when Robert the Bruce killed John, he joined Robert rather than fight him. Robert made him ambassador to the Pope in 1320 and gave him the old Macduff lands at Strathbogie in Aberdeenshire, where Huntly Castle is situated. The power of the Gordons grew until, by the 16th and 17th centuries, the Gordon chief had become known as 'The Cock o' the North'.

MODERN

MODERN DRESS

GRAHAM

Gaelic : Greumach
Motto : Ne oublie *(Do not forget)*

An Anglo-Norman family, the Grahams lived at Grey Home, mentioned in the Domesday Book until David I gave William Graham lands at Abercorn and Dunkieth. Sir John Graham of Dundaff, the 'right hand' of William Wallace, was killed at Falkirk in 1298, while John Graham of Claverhouse, known as 'Bonnie Dundee', was killed in the Pass of Killiecrankie leading the fight against William of Orange for James VII. In 1782, the then Marquis of Graham convinced Parliament to repeal the 1747 Act forbidding the wearing of Highland dress.

GRAHAM OF MENTEITH

GRAHAM OF MONTROSE

GRANT

Gaelic : Grannd
Motto : Stand fast

The name Grant comes from the French *grand*, or 'big'.
The Norman Sir William Le Grand married an Inverness-
shire heiress and by 1258 Sir Lawrence le Grand was
Sheriff of Inverness. In 1483, Sir Iain Grant married the
heiress of the Glencairies and different branches of the
Grant family come from their two sons. In 1820, the
Grant chief called out his clan by sending round the fiery
cross – the last time this was ever done – to defend his
brother, a Tory candidate in the election, who was being
threatened by supporters of the Whig candidate.

ANCIENT

WEATHERED

GUNN

Gaelic : Guinne
Motto : Aut pax aut bellum
(Either peace or war)

The Gunns were a warlike family from the north of
Scotland who were probably of Pictish origin. A
long feud began when Keith of Ackergill forced a Gunn to
marry him and she killed herself. In 1464, the Gunns
agreed to a fight with the Keiths to end the feud. There
were to be twelve horses on either side, but the Keiths
arrived with two men on each horse, killing George
Gunn, the chief, and his men. A century later George's
grandson killed 12 Keiths in revenge.

GUNN

HAMILTON

Gaelic : Hamultun
Motto : Through

The Hamiltons were originally from Leicestershire but Sir Walter Fitz-Gilbert of Hamildone was given the Barony of Cadzow for supporting Robert the Bruce and a descendant of his, James Hamilton, was made Lord Hamilton in 1445. In 1528, James's illegitimate grandson Patrick was burned to death in St Andrews for his Protestant beliefs. William, 2nd Duke of Hamilton, died just after the Battle of Worcester in 1651, and his niece Anne succeeded him. She married Lord William Douglas and the Hamilton title passed to the Douglas family.

ANCIENT GREEN

MODERN GREEN

HAY

Gaelic : Mac Garaidh
Motto : Serva jugum *(Keep the yoke)*

William de la Haye was the cupbearer of William the
Lion. He came to Scotland in 1160 and, marrying a local
Celtic heiress, was given the lands of Erroll in 1180. The
5th Hay chief was a supporter of Robert the Bruce and
saved his life. Robert gave him Slains Castle in Buchan
and made him hereditary Lord High Constable of
Scotland, commanding the king's bodyguard. James VI
eventually blew up Slains Castle in 1595, believing the
Hay chief had been plotting with his Spanish enemies. In
1633 Sir George Hay was made Earl of Kinnoul.

HAY

INNES

Gaelic : Innis
Motto : Be traist *(Be faithful)*

Beorwald Flandrensis, whose surname meant 'Flemish',
was given the Innes lands by Malcolm IV in 1160, his
grandson taking his surname from his lands. John, Bishop
of Moray (1407-14), the son of the Innes chief, rebuilt
Elgin Cathedral, which had been destroyed in 1390 by
Alexander Stewart, the evil 'Wolf of Badenoch'. The 11th
Lord of Innes, 'Ill Sir Robert', founded the Greyfriars of
Elgin as a penance for his wicked life and the 19th Lord
was obsessed by witches, claiming to have spent an
evening with the Queen of the Fairies.

INNES

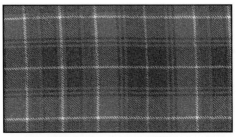

KEITH

Gaelic : Ceiteach
Motto : Veritas vincit *(Truth conquers)*

A great Celtic family, the Keiths held the office of Great Marischal and gained lands in Caithness through marriage. This led to a long feud with the Gunns who also lived in the area. In 1458 Sir William Keith was made Earl Marischal by James II, a title which gave the Keiths a great deal of influence. James, brother of the 10th Earl Marischal, became a famous soldier, taking part in the Jacobite uprising of 1715, and then rising to become both a General in the Russian army and, later, a Field-Marshal in the army of the German Frederick the Great.

ANCIENT

MODERN

KENNEDY

Gaelic : MacUalraig, Ceannaideach
Motto : Avise la fin *(Consider the end)*

The name Kennedy means 'ugly head' in Gaelic. James
Kennedy of Dunure was the second husband of Mary
Stewart, daughter of Robert III. Their youngest son
became Bishop of St Andrews, while the elder was made
Lord Kennedy in 1457. In 1509, the 3rd Lord Kennedy
was made Earl of Cassilis. Gilbert, the 4th Earl, became
notorious for roasting the Abbot of Crossraguel over a
slow fire, trying to force him to sign over lands but, in the
end, he had to let the abbot go. The Earldom of Cassilis
passed to the Kennedys of Culzean in 1759.

MODERN

WEATHERED

LAMONT

Gaelic : MacLaomainn
Motto : Ne parcas nec spernas
      (Neither spare nor dispose)

The Lamonts are descended from the original Scots who
founded the kingdom of Dalriada. They take their name
from a chief from Cowall in Argyll, in 1238, called
Ladman and their stronghold was Toward Castle. During
the Civil War, Charles I ordered Sir James Lamont to
attack the Campbell rebels in his area. In revenge, the
Campbells attacked Toward Castle, offering the Lamonts
their lives upon surrender. The Lamonts accepted, and
the Campbells treacherously killed about 200 of them.

ANCIENT

MODERN

LINDSAY

Gaelic : MacGhille Fhionntaig
Motto : Endure fort *(Endure with strength)*

A Norman, Sir Baldric de Lindsay, held lands in England
in 1086 and a William Lindsay held lands in Crawford in
1180. The Lindsays lost their English lands during the
Scottish Wars of Independence. In 1346, Sir David
Lindsay acquired Glenesk in Angus, becoming Earl of
Crawford in 1398. Marrying a daughter of Robert II he
received the Barony of Strathnairn in Inverness-shire.
Alexander, the 4th Earl, called 'Earl Beardie', opposed
James II and was defeated by the Earl of Huntly in 1452.
He lost his lands, although they were restored later.

ANCIENT

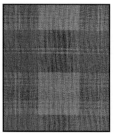

MODERN

LIVINGSTONE

Gaelic : Mac an Léigh
Motto : Si je puis *(If I can)*

The name Livingstone is said to come from a Saxon
called Leving, who lived at 'Leving's Toun' in the 12th
century. However, there are two families of Livingstones
– one of them a Lowland, the other a Highland branch.
The Highland Livingstones come from Western Argyll
and claim to be descended from a physician to one of the
Lords of the Isles. They were followers of the Stewarts of
Appin and a David Livingstone saved the banner of the
Stewarts at Culloden. Dr David Livingstone, the explorer,
(1813-73) descended from the Highland branch.

ANCIENT

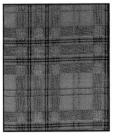

MODERN

MacAlister

Gaelic : MacAlasdair
Motto : Fortiter *(Boldly)*

The MacAlisters are a branch of Clan Donald. Their
founder, Alasdair Mor, was the younger son of Donald of
Islay, himself the great-grandson of the mighty King
Somerled. He died in 1299 fighting against Alasdair
MacDougall, Lord of Lorn. The MacAlister lands were
mainly in Kintyre and, in 1481, Charles Macallestar was
made Steward of Kintyre. Their stronghold was a castle
on Loch Tarbert and the main branch of the family are
the MacAlisters of Loup. Arran members of the
MacAlisters formed a group called Clann Allaster Beg.

MacAlister

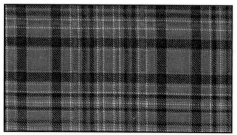

MacAulay

Gaelic : MacAmhlaidh
Motto : Dulce periculum *(Danger is sweet)*

There are two MacAulay clans, who are unrelated to each other. The Gaelic MacAulays are descended from Aulay, a younger son of Alwin, the Earl of Lennox in 1200. Their lands were mainly in Dunbartonshire and they were known as the MacAulays of Ardencaple. Eventually Ardencaple Castle was sold by the 12th chief, to repay debts, in 1767. The Norse MacAulays are based in Lewis, Sutherland and Ross-shire, and claim to be descended from Olave the Black, the last king of Man and the Isles. They were followers of the MacLeods.

ANCIENT HUNTING

MODERN HUNTING

45

MacCallum

Gaelic : MacChauluim
Motto : In ardua petit
    (He has attempted difficult things)

A Gaelic clan, the MacCallum lands were originally in Lorne in Argyll. Their name means 'son of Columba', the saint who landed in Scotland in 593, but it was often anglicised to Malcolm, which comes from *Maol Chaluim* or 'follower of Columba'. In 1414, Duncan Campbell of Lochow granted the Craignish lands at Loch Avich to Reginald MacCallum, and made him Constable of the Castles of Lachaffy and Craignish. Dugald Malcolm of Poltalloch inherited the estates in 1779.

ANCIENT

MODERN

MacDonald

Gaelic : MacDhòmhnuill
Motto : Per mare per terras
(By sea and by land)

The name MacDonald comes from Donald of Islay, King
of the Isles and grandson of Somerled, who fought for
independence from Norway and died in 1164. Once one
of the most powerful clans in Scotland, the MacDonalds
were kings in their own right. Their lands included all of
the Hebrides, Mull, Uist, Barra, Skye, Lewis and a great
deal of Ross and Inverness-shire. They lost the lordship
of the Isles and their lands in Ross in the 15th century
but the present chief still holds lands in Skye.

ANCIENT

MODERN

MacDougall

Gaelic : MacDhùghaill
Motto : Buaidh no bàs *(To conquer or die)*

The MacDougalls are descended from Dougall, the eldest
son of Somerled. His grandson married a sister of John
Comyn and, when Robert the Bruce killed John's son, the
'Red Comyn', in Dumfries, the MacDougalls became his
bitter enemies. After Bannockburn Robert took the
MacDougall lands, but the 7th chief married Robert's
granddaughter and David II returned the lands of Lorn
to their son. In 1388, John MacDougall of Lorn died
without a male heir and his lands passed to the Stewarts
through his daughters.

DOUGALL

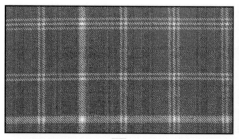

MACDUFF

Gaelic : MacDhuibh
Motto : Deus juvat *(God assists)*

The name MacDuff means 'son of the dark one' and the MacDuffs are descended from the same ancient royal house as Shakespeare's Macbeth. Traditionally, MacDuff was the first Earl of Fife, who opposed Macbeth and helped Malcolm to the throne. The MacDuffs, under their earl, had the privilege of crowning the king and of always being in the front ranks of his army – a position of great honour. In 1306, Robert the Bruce had Duncan MacDuff, Earl of Fife, imprisoned for 7 years, as he had been a supporter of the Comyns.

ANCIENT HUNTING

MODERN DRESS

MacEwen

Gaelic : MacEòghainn
Motto : Reviresco (*I grow strong*)

Ewen of Otter, who lived at the beginning of the 13th
century, was the founder of the MacEwen clan and there
were 9 chiefs until the last MacEwen of Otter, Swene
MacEwen. Their lands were at Loch Fyne and their castle
was near Kilfinan. Swene gave some of the Otter lands to
Duncan Campbell in 1432 and, in 1523, James V gave
Colin Campbell, the Earl of Argyll, the barony of Otter.
With no lands the MacEwens became a 'broken clan'.
Some became bards to the Campbells, while others were
forced to disperse and live as best they could.

MacEwen

MacFarlane

Gaelic : MacPhàrlain
Motto : This I'll defend

Bartholemew *(Parlan* in Gaelic), the founder of the clan, was the great grandson of Gilchrist, a brother of the Earl of Lennox in the 13th century. Duncan, the 6th chief, was given lands on the north banks of Loch Lomond by the Earl of Lennox and, in 1395, gained more lands through marriage. After an earl of Lennox was beheaded in 1425 the MacFarlanes should have been given the title, but Sir John Stewart of Darnley became earl. A feud began that lasted until a MacFarlane eventually married the daughter of a later Stewart earl of Lennox.

MODERN

WEATHERED

MACFIE

Gaelic : MacDubh-shithe
Motto : Pro rege *(For the king)*

The Macfies or Macduffies are a branch of Clan Alpine, descended from Kenneth MacAlpine. Their Gaelic name *Dubh-shithe* means 'dark, peaceful one' and their lands were on the islands of Colonsay and Oronsay. They were hereditary keepers of the records of the Isles. In 1623, Malcolm Macfie was killed with many of his men by Coll Kitto MacDonald, who took Colonsay for himself. Now a 'broken clan', some Macfies followed MacDonald of Islay, while others moved to Lochaber to follow Cameron of Lochiel, joining his clan at Culloden.

MACFIE

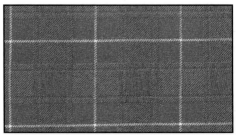

MACGREGOR

Gaelic : MacGrioghair
Motto : 'S rioghal mo dhream
     (Royal is my race)

The Macgregors, or 'The Children of the Mist', are a branch of Clan Alpine, descended from Griogar, son of Alpin, 8th century King of Dalriada. Alexander II gave them land on the Perth/Argyll borders after they helped him conquer Argyll in 1221. The Campbells believed that this land was rightfully theirs and the Macgregors often had to fight to defend it. The Macgregors were outlawed after a fight with the Colquhouns in 1603 and, until 1775, the penalty for even being called Macgregor was death.

ANCIENT HUNTING

MODERN

MACINTYRE

Gaelic : Mac an t-Saoir
Motto : Per ardua *(Through difficulties)*

The Gaelic name of this clan, *Mac an t-Saoir*, means 'son of the carpenter', and the clan originally held lands in Kintyre, Glenoe and Badenoch. The Macintyres of Glenoe were hereditary forresters to the Stewart Lords of Lorn. Another branch were hereditary bards to the Menzies chiefs and to MacDonald of Clanranald. Donnachadh Ban Mac an t-Saoir was a forrester. He fought against the Jacobites at Culloden, but was later imprisoned for writing a poem criticising the 1747 Act which forbade the wearing of Highland dress.

ANCIENT HUNTING

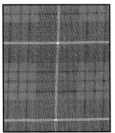

WEATHERED HUNTING

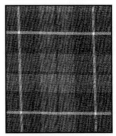

MACKAY

Gaelic : MacAoidh
Motto : Manu forti *(With a strong hand)*

The Mackays claim descent from the Royal House of
Moray. They are known as Clan Morgan, from a 14th
century Morgan, son of Magnus, and as Clan Aoidh,
from Morgan's grandson. From about 1160, a large part
of the clan lived in Ross and Sutherland, where they
supported Angus Dubh against the Lord of the Isles in
the 15th century. After this time the power of the clan
declined until the last lands were sold in 1829 to the
Sutherland family. Many Mackays suffered during the
Highland Clearances.

ANCIENT BLUE

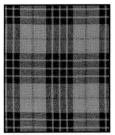

MODERN

MACKENZIE

Gaelic : MacCoinnich
Motto : Luceo non uro *(I shine, not burn)*

The Celtic Mackenzies are descended from Coinnich, ('bright one' in Gaelic), the grandson of Colin, who died in 1278 and from whom the earls of Ross are descended. David II gave Murdoch, son of Kenneth, the lands of Kintail in 1362. In 1623, James VI made Colin Mackenzie the Earl of Seaforth. The 5th Earl lost his title and estates fighting for James Stuart, the Old Pretender, at the Battle of Sheriffmuir in 1715. Kenneth, the 5th Earl's grandson, repurchased his lands and was restored to the Seaforth title in 1771. In 1778 he raised the Seaforth Highlanders.

ANCIENT

MODERN

MACKINNON

Gaelic : MacFhionghuin
Motto : Audentes fortuna juvat
(Fortune assists the daring)

The MacKinnons, also known as Clan Fingon, are a branch of Clan Alpine, descended from Fingon, Kenneth MacAlpine's great-grandson. Their lands were on Mull and Skye and they were custodians of the standards of weights and measures for the Lords of the Isles. In 1650 they fought at the Battle of Worcester, and, in 1715, John Dhu MacKinnon fought at Sheriffmuir. The MacKinnon chief was imprisoned after Culloden, but was eventually released because of his old age and bad health.

ANCIENT HUNTING

MODERN HUNTING

MACKINTOSH

Gaelic : Mac an Toisich
Motto : Touch not the cat bot a glove
(Touch not the cat without a glove)

Mac an Toisich means 'son of the chief', and the first
Mackintosh was said to be the son of a MacDuff, the clan
who were the ancestors of the Earls of Fife. The 6th
Laird, Angus, married the heiress of Clan Chattan in
1291, becoming its chief. Angus later supported Robert
the Bruce in his fight against the Comyns. In 1745,
Angus, the then chief, fought with the Black Watch on
the side of the Government but his wife, 'Colonel Anne'
Farquharson raised the clan for Prince Charles.

ANCIENT RED

MODERN RED

MacLachlan

Gaelic : Mac Lachlainn
Motto : Fortis et fidus *(Brave and trusty)*

The MacLachlans are a Celtic clan, and claim descent from the ancient Irish Kings, although their name comes from *Lochlann*, which is 'Norway' in Gaelic. Their lands were at Strathlachlan, near Loch Fyne. The MacLachlans were followers of the Lords of the Isles, but later the MacLachlans of Coire-unan became standard bearers to Cameron of Lochiel. In 1689, the MacLachlans fought at Killiecrankie with Viscount Dundee. Chief Lachlan MacLachlan and his son both died at Culloden but Robert MacLachlan regained the family estates in 1749.

ANCIENT

WEATHERED

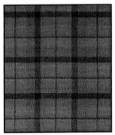

MACLAREN

Gaelic : MacLabhruinn
Motto : Creag an Turie *(The boar's rock)*

The MacLarens claim descent from Lorn, son of Erc, who came to Scotland in 503. In any case, by the 12th century they had lands in Balquhidder and Strathearn. In the 14th century, the MacLarens lost the lands of Strathearn to the Crown, but continued to be loyal, fighting for James III at Sauchieburn in 1488, at Flodden in 1513 for James IV, and at Pinkie Cleugh for Mary, Queen of Scots in 1547. The clan also fought at Culloden, where MacLaren of Invernenty was taken prisoner, although he later managed to escape.

ANCIENT

MODERN

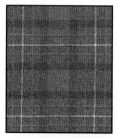

MACLEAN

Gaelic : MacGhille Eoin
Motto : Virtue mine honour

The Macleans are descended from Gillean of the Battle Axe. The main branch, the Macleans of Duart, are descended from his son Lachlan Lubonach and had lands on Mull and other Western Isles. They followed the MacDougalls of Lorn and the Lords of the Isles until the lordship was abolished. One chief, Lachlan Maclean, married the sister of Campbell of Argyll. As she was childless, he had her tied to a rock, hoping that the tide would drown her. She was saved by a fisherman and Lachlan was killed by her brother in Edinburgh in 1523.

MACLEAN OF DUART

MACLAINE OF LOCHBUIE

MacLeod

Gaelic : MacLeòd
Motto : Hold fast

The MacLeods are descended from Leod, son of the 13th century Olave the Black, King of Man. The main branch is called Clan Tormod from Leod's son. With lands on St Kilda, Harris and Skye, the MacLeods were at war with the MacDonalds for a long time. They supported Charles I and Charles II but, as they were practically wiped out at the Battle of Worcester in 1651, they did not take part in the Jacobite risings. Their castle, Dunvegan Castle on Skye, has been continuously inhabited by their chiefs, the MacLeods of MacLeod, for over 20 generations.

ANCIENT HARRIS

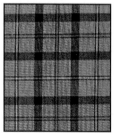

MODERN HARRIS

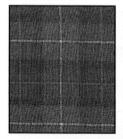

MACMILLAN

Gaelic : MacGhille-Mhaolain
Motto : Miseris succurrere disco
     (I learn to succour the distressed)

The Gaelic name of *Mac Mhaolain*, 'the son of the bald one', or tonsured priest, suggests that the Macmillans are related to one of the old Celtic monastic families. Malcolm Mor Macmillan was granted a charter, in 1390, from the Lord of the Isles to lands at Knapdale for 'so long as the wave beats on the rock'. The clan lost most of their lands in the 15th century. Harold Macmillan was prime minister from 1957-63. Kirkpatrick Macmillan (1813-78) invented the pedal bicycle.

ANCIENT HUNTING

MODERN OLD

MACNAB

Gaelic : Mac an Aba
Motto : Timor omnis abesto
(Let fear be far from all)

The Macnabs are a branch of Clan Alpine, known as
Clann-an-Aba, the clan of the Abbot, and are descended
from the abbots of Glendochart, although their line may
go back to St Fillan mac Feradach, of the house of Lorn,
who died in 793. The clan supported the MacDougalls
against Robert the Bruce at Bannockburn in 1314, losing
most of their lands, except the Barony of Bowain, which
David II confirmed as theirs in 1336. In 1746, the chief
fought for the Government, his clan for Prince Charles.

MACNAB

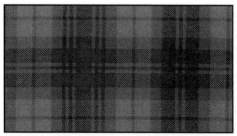

MacNaughton

Gaelic : MacNeachdainn
Motto : I hope in God

An ancient clan, the name *Neachdainn*, which means
'pure one' in Gaelic, can be traced back to the Pictish
Kings of Bude. Gilchrist MacNaughton was made keeper
of the castle of Fraoch Eilean on Loch Awe in 1267 and
the clan also held the castles of Dubh-Loch in Glenshira
and Dunderave on Loch Fyne. They lost many of their
lands after Bannockburn, having opposed Robert the
Bruce, but David II granted them lands in Lewis. After
fighting for Dundee at the battle of Killiecrankie the clan
lost their estates again in 1689.

MODERN

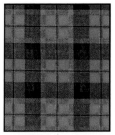

WEATHERED

MacNeil

Gaelic : MacNèill
Motto : Vincere vel mori
    (To conquer or die)

The MacNeils are a Celtic clan and claim descent from the Irish High King Niall of the Nine Hostages who came to Barra in 1049. As a follower of the Lord of the Isles, Gilleonan MacNeil was officially granted Barra and lands in South Uist in 1427, and this was confirmed by James IV in 1495. Later, the MacNeils of Barra followed the Macleans of Duart, often having to fight the MacNeils of Gigha, their kinsmen, who supported the MacDonalds of Islay, the Macleans' sworn enemies.

MacNeil of Barra

MacNeil of Colonsay

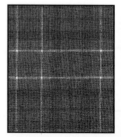

MACPHERSON

Gaelic : Mac a' Phearsoin, MacMhuirich
Motto : Touch not the cat bot a glove
(Touch not the cat without a glove)

The Macphersons are descendants of Muriach, chief of
Clan Chattan in 1178 and, later, a 15th-century parson of
Kingussie, *Mac a'Phearsoin* meaning 'son of the parson'.
The Macphersons had a long feud with the Mackintoshes
over the Clan Chattan leadership. The Macphersons of
Cluny are the main branch of the family. In 1745, Ewen
Macpherson of Cluny joined Prince Charles. Having
helped the Prince, he went into hiding for 9 years, getting
to France in 1755 with a price of £1000 on his head.

ANCIENT RED

MODERN HUNTING

MACQUARRIE

Gaelic : MacGuadhre
Motto : An t'Arm breac dearg
     (The red tartaned army)

The Macquarries are a branch of Clan Alpine. Their founder, Guaire, which means 'noble', was the brother of Fingon, ancestor of the Makinnons. John Macquarrie held lands on the Hebridean islands of Uist and Mull in 1473. When the lordship of the Isles was abolished, the Macquarries became followers of the Macleans. In 1651, Allan Macquarrie and many members of his clan were killed fighting at the Battle of Inverkeithing for Charles II against the troops of Oliver Cromwell.

MACQUARRIE

MACRAE

Gaelic : MacRath
Motto : Fortitudine *(With fortitude)*

MacRath means 'the son of grace'. The Macraes had lands in Kintail from about the 14th century, although they had other lands in Beuly, Conchra and Ardachy. They were a warlike clan who were known as the 'Wild Macraes'. They were supporters of the Mackenzies, who made them hereditary constables of Eilean Donan Castle, and they became famous as 'Mackenzie's coat of mail'. The Macraes fought for James Stuart, the Old Pretender, at the Battle of Sheriffmuir in 1715, but they did not take part at Culloden.

MODERN DRESS

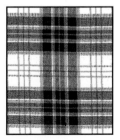

MACRAE PRINCESS

MAXWELL

Motto : Reviresco
     (I flourish again)

The Maxwells were a powerful Borders family who are
descended from either the 11th-century Maccus, King of
Man, or from a Norman family. Their name comes from
'Maccus's Wiel' a pool on the River Tweed near Kelso.
Herbert Maxwell of Caerlaverock was made Lord
Maxwell in 1445 and, in 1581, the then chief was made
Earl of Morton. The 5th Earl of Morton was a Jacobite
and was captured at Preston in 1715. He was taken to the
Tower of London, but escaped on the day he was to be
beheaded, disguised as a serving maid.

MAXWELL

MENZIES

Gaelic : Méinn, Méinnearach
Motto : Will God I shall

The Menzies (pronounced Mingiz) are a Norman family, who came from the town of Mesnières, near Rouen in Normandy. Sir Robert de Menyers became Lord High Chamberlain of Scotland in 1249. His son, Alexander, was given the lands of Weem in Perthshire by the Earl of Atholl, and Robert the Bruce gave him more lands after the Battle of Bannockburn. In 1423, David Menzies was made Governor of Orkney and Shetland, while Sir Alexander Menzies of Castle Menzies was made Baronet of Nova Scotia in 1665.

RED AND WHITE

BLACK AND WHITE

MORRISON

Gaelic : MacGhille Mhoire
Motto : Dun Eistein *(Castle Eistein)*

There are various families of Morrisons in Scotland. The
Highland Morrisons, whose name means 'the son of the
servant of Mary', may be descended from the illegitimate
son of a Norse king, who was shipwrecked with his family
off Lewis. The Morrisons came to hold the hereditary
office of brieve, or judge, in Lewis and by the 16th century the then Morrison chief, Hugh Morrison, was brieve,
holding Castle Eistein. The Morrisons feuded with the
MacLeods, but by about 1615 had ceased to be brieves or
to hold as much power as before.

ANCIENT RED

MODERN GREEN

MUNRO

Gaelic : Mac an Rothaich
Motto : Dread God

The home of the Munros is the land called Ferindonald,
'the land of Donald', after the founder of the clan, and
lies in Easter Ross, opposite the Black Isle. The first
Munro of Foulis was Hugh Munro, who died in 1126, and
the present chief still lives at Castle Foulis. The Munros
supported the government in the Jacobite risings, and
took part in the 30 Years War on the Protestant side.
General Sir Hector Munro (1726-1805), had a folly built
on the top of a local hill, Cnoc Fyrish, which is said to be
a copy of the gates of Hyderabad in India.

ANCIENT

MODERN

MURRAY

Gaelic : MacMhuirich
Motto : Tout prêt *(Quite ready)*

The Murrays are descended from a Pictish tribe that lived
in the Province of Moray. The main branch of the family
is descended from Freskin de Moravia, who was given
lands in Moray by David I. His grandson, William, married the heiress of Bothwell, and became the ancestor of
the Murrays of Tullibardine and of the Dukes of Atholl.
The Murrays fought with William Wallace under Sir
Andrew Murray at the Battle of Stirling Bridge in 1297.
Sir Andrew's son, another Andrew, was Regent of
Scotland after Robert the Bruce's death in 1329.

ANCIENT ATHOLL

MODERN ATHOLL

OGILVIE

Gaelic : Mac Ghille Bhuidhe
Motto : À fin *(To the end)*

The name Ogilvie comes from the Brythonic *Ocel Fa*, or 'high plain', and the clan are descended from Gillibride, second son of Gillechrist, Earl of Angus. William the Lion gave him the barony of Ogilvie in 1163. The clan were supporters of both Charles I and Charles II and, in 1645, James Ogilvie, 2nd Earl of Airlie, was imprisoned but managed to escape dressed in his sister's clothes. The Ogilvies fought for the Jacobites in 1715 and again in 1745/6. David, 5th Lord Ogilvie, escaped to France after Culloden, but returned in 1783, having been pardoned.

ANCIENT OLD AND RARE

ANCIENT AIRLIE

RAMSAY

Gaelic : Ramsaidh
Motto : Ora et labora *(Pray and work)*

The Ramsays are of Norman origin and the name means
'wild garlic island'. Simon of Ramsay was given lands in
Lothian by David I, and was the ancestor of the Ramsays
of Dalhousie. The Ramsays fought in the border wars
with England and an Alexander Ramsay was made
Sheriff of Teviotdale in 1388 after successfully defending
Dunbar. Unfortunately the previous sheriff, Sir William
Douglas, was so annoyed by this that he captured and
imprisoned Alexander, starving him to death. William
Ramsay was made Earl of Dalhousie in 1633.

MODERN RED

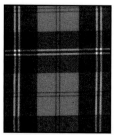

MODERN BLUE

ROBERTSON

Gaelic : Mac Raibeirt
Motto : Virtutis gloria merces
(Glory is the reward of valour)

The Robertsons, who are known as Clan Donnachaidh,
are descended from Donnachadh Reamhar, Duncan the
Fat, a friend of Robert the Bruce who led the clan at
Bannockburn. The clan's name comes from Robert
Riach, Grizzled Robert, who caught the murderers of
James I. Chief Alexander Robertson renounced his job
as a clergyman to fight with Viscount Dundee in 1688,
and again with the Jacobites in 1715. His clan fought at
Culloden, but he himself was by then too old.

MODERN HUNTING

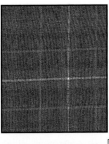

MODERN RED

ROSE

Gaelic : Ròis
Motto : Constant and true

The son of Hugh Rose of Geddes, whose ancestors had
come to England from Normandy with Bishop Odo of
Bayeux, acquired the lands of Kilravock by marriage in
the 12th century. The Rose clan remained loyal to the
Government during the Jacobite rebellions but, even so,
Prince Charles, the Young Pretender, was entertained at
their stronghold of Kilravock Castle in Nairn, shortly
before Culloden. Sir Hugh Rose was made Baron
Strathnairn in 1866 after successfully commanding a force
during the Indian Mutiny.

ANCIENT HUNTING

MODERN HUNTING

ROSS

Gaelic : Clann Andrias
Motto : Spem successus alit
(Success nourishes hope)

Of a different ancestry to the Roses, the Rosses, called in
Gaelic *Clann Andrias*, take their name from the province
from whence they come. An important early chief,
Fearchar Mac-an-t-Saigairt, the 'son of the priest', was a
supporter of Alexander II, who made him Earl of Ross in
1234. Another chief, William Ross, fought at the Battle of
Bannockburn, but the earldom passed to the Lords of the
Isles, and to the Crown in 1476, on the death of a later
William Ross. Dick Ross is a well-known writer.

ANCIENT HUNTING

WEATHERED HUNTING

SCOTT

Gaelic : Scot, Scotach
Motto : Amo *(I love)*

Powerful in the Borders and Fife, the Scott clan take their name from the *Scotii*, who came over from Ireland in the 6th century. Two important branches, the Scotts of Buccleuch and the Scotts of Balwearie, descend from Sir Richard and Sir Michael, two sons of Uchtredus filius Scoti, or 'son of the Scot', who lived early in the 12th century. A later Sir Michael Scott, who died around 1300, was known as 'The Wizard' for his interest in magic and alchemy, but the most famous Scott was Sir Walter Scott, the writer, who helped romanticize the image of Scotland.

ANCIENT

MODERN RED

SCRYMGEOUR

Motto : Dissipate

The name Scrymgeour comes from the Old French *eskermisor*, skirmisher or sword fencer, and the Scrymgeours are of Norman origin. They had been hereditary standard bearers to the king since Alexander II's day and, in 1298, William Wallace and Robert the Bruce granted Alexander Schrymeschur lands near Dundee and made him Constable of Dundee Castle in two charters. Alexander was hanged by Edward I in 1306. In 1370, a later Alexander married Agnes, the heiress of Glassary in Argyll, and the Scrymgeours gained those lands.

SCRYMGEOUR

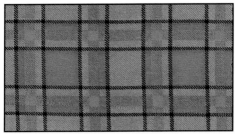

SHAW

Gaelic : Mac Ghille-Sheathanaich
Motto : Fide et fortitudine
(By fidelity and fortitude)

The Shaws were important members of Clan Chattan
who were descended from the Mackintosh chiefs in the
14th century. Farquhart Shaw, great-grandson of Angus,
6th Chief of Mackintosh, was given the lands of
Rothiermurchus after leading Clan Chattan at the great
clan battle that took place on the North Inch near Perth
in 1396. Farquhart's son, James, was killed at the Battle
of Harlaw and so his grandson, Alasdair Giar, succeeded
to his lands, which were sold in the 16th century.

ANCIENT

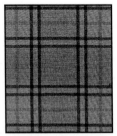

MODERN

SINCLAIR

Gaelic : Mac na Ceardadh
Motto : Commit thy work to God

William de Sancto Claro, whose family came from St Claire-sur-Elle in Normandy, was given the barony of Roslin in Midlothian in the 12th century. Sir Henry St Clair supported Robert the Bruce and his son, Sir William, joined Sir James Douglas in carrying Robert's heart to the Holy Land. He was killed fighting the Moors in Spain. In 1379, a later Sir Henry Sinclair became Earl of Orkney by marrying Isabella, Countess of Orkney, an earldom which James III bought from him in 1470. William, the 3rd Earl, became Earl of Caithness in 1455.

ANCIENT HUNTING

MODERN HUNTING

STEWART

Gaelic : Stiubhard
Motto : Virescit vulnere virtus
  (Courage grows strong at a wound)

The ancestor of the Stewarts was Walter Fitz-Allan, an Anglo-Norman knight who was given land and made High Steward of Scotland by David I, a title which Malcolm IV confirmed as hereditary. Many noble families have come from the Stewarts and, as a result of the marriage of Walter, 6th High Steward, to Marjory, daughter of Robert the Bruce, there have been 14 Stewarts on the throne from Robert II who began his reign in 1371 to Queen Anne, who died in 1714.

STEWART

MODERN ROYAL STEWART

SUTHERLAND

Gaelic : Sutherlarach
Motto : Sans peur *(Without fear)*

The Sutherlands are Celts from the region of Scotland
known to the Vikings as *Sudrland* – the South Land.
William, Lord of Sutherland was given the earldom of
Sutherland in 1228. The 2nd Earl fought at Bannockburn,
and the 4th Earl married a daughter of Robert the Bruce.
The Sutherlands had many feuds, particularly with the
Mackays. Their chief lived at Dunrobin Castle in Golspie.
In the 16th century, the earldom passed to Adam
Gordon, who had married a daughter of the old earl and
disinherited the rightful heirs.

ANCIENT OLD

MODERN OLD

URQUHART

Gaelic : Urchurdan
Motto : Mean, speak and do weil

The name Urquhart comes from Castle Urquhart on the banks of Loch Ness. In 1358, William Urquhart was made Sheriff of Cromarty by Robert the Bruce. The most famous Urquhart was Sir Thomas Urquhart of Cromarty, who translated Rabelais. He died of laughter in 1660, hearing news of the Restoration of the monarchy. Although the clan were ancient, they were not as ancient as Sir Thomas claimed when he decided that he was 143rd in direct descent from the biblical Adam. The last of the male line, Colonel James Urquhart, died in 1741.

URQUHART

WALLACE

Gaelic : Uallas
Motto : Pro libertate *(For liberty)*

Wallace comes from the Medieval Latin *Wallensis*, which means Welsh, but which was used in Scotland to describe the Welsh, or British, of the Strathclyde region. A Richard Wallace, who lived in the 12th century, obtained lands in Ayrshire. His great-great-grandson was the famous Scottish hero William Wallace (1274-1305). William led resistance against the English, his guerrilla tactics gaining more and more support from the Scottish nobles as time went on. Eventually, William was betrayed and taken to London where Edward I had him executed.

ANCIENT HUNTING

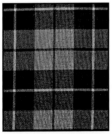

MODERN

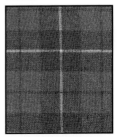

843 Kenneth MacAlpine unites the kingdoms of Dalriada and Pictland into the kingdom of Alba.

1018 Malcolm II beats the Angles at Carnham, bringing Lothian into Alba.

1040 Duncan I is killed by MacBeth, Mormaer (Earl) of Moray.

1057 Malcolm Canmore kills MacBeth, to become Malcolm III.

1124 David I becomes king, and gives many lands to his Anglo-Norman followers.

1164 Somerled, king of Argyll and some of the Western Isles, is killed at Renfrew.

1263 The Norse are defeated at Largs. Soon afterwards, the remaining Western Isles and the Isle of Man are given to Scotland.

1292 The Maid of Norway, the last descendant of Malcolm Canmore, dies. John Balliol is chosen as king.

1296 Edward I of England deposes Balliol. Many Scots sign the Ragman Rolls, swearing allegiance to Edward.

1298 The independence movement of William Wallace is defeated at Falkirk, and Wallace is executed in London.

1306 Robert the Bruce kills his rival John, the Red Comyn, becoming king. When Edward I defeats him, he escapes abroad.

1314 Robert defeats Edward II at Bannockburn.

1371 After Robert's son dies, Robert Stewart becomes Robert II.

1390 Robert III is king, but the Duke of Albany has the real power.

1406 Robert sends his son, James, aged 11, to France, but he is captured by the English. Robert dies.

1424 James I is freed, and returns to Scotland to overthrow the Duke of Albany.

1437 James I is murdered. James II is only 6.

1449 James II begins to rule Scotland.

1460 James II dies taking Roxburgh. James III is only 9. He marries the King of Norway's daughter. Her dowry includes Orkney and the Shetland Islands.

1488 James III dies at Sauchieburn. James IV is crowned at 15.

1503 James IV marries Margaret Tudor.

1513 James IV dies at Flodden. James V is only 5 months old.

1542 James V dies at Solway Moss. His daughter, Mary, is a baby. The Earl of Arran becomes Regent. Henry VIII wants Mary to marry his son Edward, but instead Arran sends her to France.

1547 The Scots are defeated at Pinkie Cleugh by the Duke of Somerset.

1554 Arran resigns, Marie de Guise becomes Regent. Some lords declare themselves Protestant 'Lords of the Congregation'.

1560 Marie de Guise dies.

1561 Back from France, Mary, Queen of Scots, lands at Leith.

1567 Mary abdicates in favour of her baby son, James VI. She flees to England where Elizabeth I imprisons her and eventually has her beheaded.

1603 James VI inherits the English throne as James I.

1625 James dies and his son, Charles I, succeeds him.

1638 Many Scots sign the National Covenant, condemning English Protestantism.

1649 Oliver Cromwell has Charles executed. The Scots invite Charles II to become king but Cromwell forces him into exile.

1660 After Cromwell dies, Charles II is made king. In secret, the Covenanters worship in 'coventicles'.

1670 Coventicles are declared to be treasonable and many Covenanters are slaughtered.

1685 Charles II dies and is succeeded by his Catholic brother, James VII/II.

1688 William of Orange and Mary, James' daughter, are crowned King and Queen after James is deposed.

1689 The Jacobites, Scots loyal to James, rise up under 'Bonnie Dundee'. They defeat the English at Killiecrankie but Dundee is killed.

1692 Soldiers carry out the Massacre of Glencoe after Alisdair MacIain of Clan Donald cannot swear allegiance to the king on time.

1707 The Treaty of Union joins the English and Scottish parliaments.

1708 James Edward Stuart, the Old Pretender, makes the first of three attempts to regain the throne.

1745 Prince Charles Edward Stuart, the Young Pretender, lands in Scotland. He defeats General Cope at Prestonpans but the Duke of Cumberland defeats his smaller army at Culloden in 1746. Escaping, Charles dies in Rome.

1747 The Act of Proscription bans Highland dress.

1780 The Highland Clearances begin. Thousands of Highlanders are evicted or forced to emigrate abroad to escape poverty.

SCOTTISH MONARCHS

843-58 Kenneth MacAlpine

858-62 Donald I

862-77 Constantine I

877-78 Aed

878-89 Eochaid and Giric

889-900 Donald II

900-43 Constantine II

943-54 Malcolm I

954-62 Indulf

962-66 Dubh

966-71 Culen

971-95 Kenneth II

995-97 Constantine III

997-1005 Kenneth III

1005-34 Malcolm II

1034-40 Duncan

1040-57 Macbeth

1058 Lulach

1058-93 Malcolm III, Canmore

1093-4 Donald III, Bane

1094 Duncan II

1094-1107 Donald III, Bane

1107-24 Alexander I

1124-53 David I

1153-65 Malcolm IV, the Maiden

1165-1214 William I, the Lion

1214-49 Alexander II

1249-86 Alexander III

1286-90 Margaret, the Maid of Norway

1292-96 John Balliol

1296-1306 Interregnum
1306-29 Robert I, the Bruce
1329-71 David II

Stewart
1371-90 Robert II
1390-1406 Robert III
1406-37 James I
1437-60 James II
1460-88 James III
1488-1513 James IV
1513-42 James V
1542-67 Mary
1567-1625 James VI/I
1625-49 Charles I
1649-60 The Commonwealth
1660-85 Charles II
1685-88 James VII/II

1688-94 William and Mary
1694-1702 William (alone)
1702-1714 Anne

Hanover
1714-27 George I
1727-60 George II
1760-1820 George III
1820-30 George IV
1830-37 William II/IV

Saxe-Coburg-Gotha
1837-1901 Victoria
1901-10 Edward I/VII

Windsor
1910-36 George V
1936 Edward II/VIII
1936-52 George VI
1952- Elizabeth I/II

TITLES IN THIS SERIES INCLUDE:

ASTRONOMY

CARD GAMES

CLANS & TARTANS

FASTEST CARS

FLAGS OF THE WORLD

HANDGUNS & SMALL ARMS

HISTORIC BRITAIN

HUMAN BODY

INVENTIONS

NATURAL DISASTERS